WHY BED BUGS BITE

and Other Gross Facts about Bugs

by Jody Sullivan Rake

Consultant: Rayda K. Krell, PhD
Entomology and Integrated Pest Management Consultant
New Canaan, Connecticut

CAPSTONE PRESS
a capstone imprint

First Facts is published by Capstone Press,
1710 Roe Crest Drive, North Mankato, Minnesota 56003.
www.capstonepub.com

Books published by Capstone Press are manufactured with paper
containing at least 10 percent post-consumer waste.

Library of Congress Cataloging-in-Publication Data
Rake, Jody Sullivan.
  Why bed bugs bite and other gross facts about bugs / by Jody Sullivan Rake.
     p. cm. — (First facts. gross me out.)
  Summary: "Describes unusual bugs, including dung beetles, millipedes,
and bed bugs"—Provided by publisher.
Includes bibliographical references and index.
  ISBN 978-1-4296-7612-0 (library binding)
  ISBN 978-1-4296-7954-1 (paperback)
  1. Insects—Miscellanea—Juvenile literature. 2. Bed bugs—Juvenile literature. I. Title.
  QL467.2.R35 2012
  595.7'54—dc23   2011033930

Editorial Credits
Mari Bolte, editor; Veronica Correia, designer; Marcie Spence, media researcher;
    Kathy McColley, production specialist

Image Credits
Alamy Images: Gustavo Mazzarollo, 21, Tim Graham, 17; AP Images: PRNewsFoto/
Orkin, LLC, 15; Shutterstock: 3drenderings, 12, Alexey U, 9, Artur Tiutenko, cover (bug),
14, beltsazar, 8, Denis Barbulat, 7 (bottom), DVARG, 3, 6, Four Oaks, 11, iliuta goean,
13, Kelly Hironaka, 16, KRSTSEVA, 4, Mr. Green, 19 (top), Pasi Koskela, 5, Potapov
Alexander, 20-21, Serg64, 7 (top), Sergey Mikhaylov, 18, Skryl, 10, Socrates, 19 (bottom),
William Attard McCarthy, cover (skin)

Printed in the United States of America in North Mankato, Minnesota.

012013   007156R

TABLE OF CONTENTS

That's So Gross!

Blood Suckers

Mosquitoes don't just suck your blood. They also spit into the bite. And that's not all. Sometimes mosquitoes can pick up disease-causing agents from other animals. Then they poke the germs right into you. So be sure to wear bug spray!

Gross Fact!

In Africa germ-carrying
mosquitoes kill more people
than any other animal.

There's a Fly on Your Food

There's a good reason people say, "Shoo, fly!" Some flies will eat anything, even poop. That poop is still on their legs and bodies when they land on your lunch. Flies **digest** their meals by spitting stomach juices onto their food. Then they suck up the food. Slurp!

digest—to break down food so it can be used by the body

Gross Fact!

Some flies also lay their eggs in dead animals. Maggots hatch from the eggs. The maggots feed on the dead body.

She Mates, Then Kills

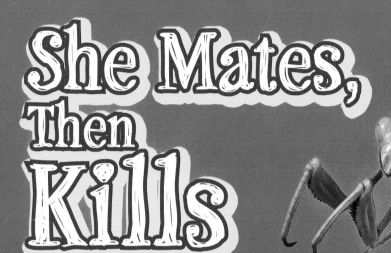

Do you think praying mantids look scary? They are if you are an insect! When a female praying mantid is hungry, she can't wait to eat. She sometimes bites off her mate's head. Then she eats him!

mantid—the common name for a group of insects, including those with the scientific name *Mantis*; these insects have triangular heads and front legs used for grasping prey.

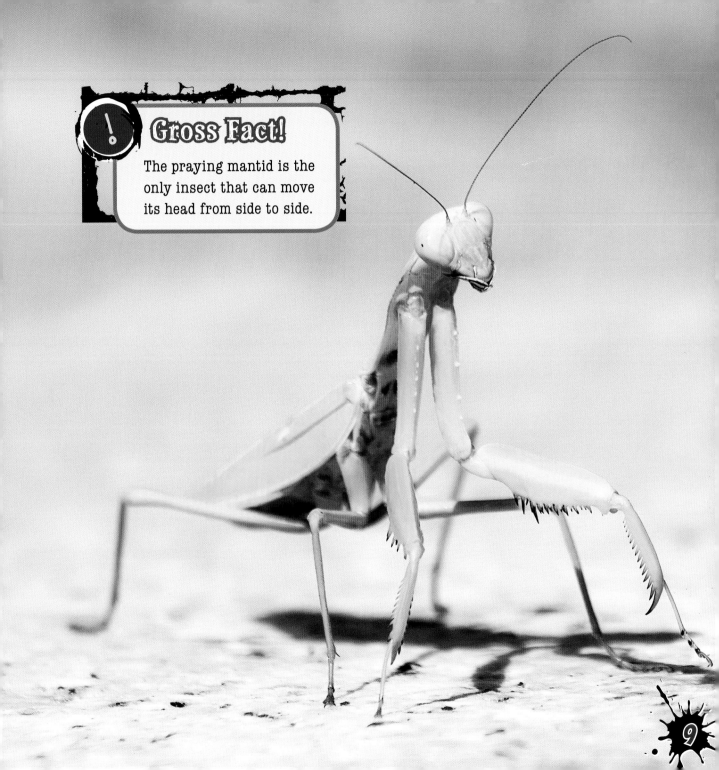

Gross Fact!

The praying mantid is the only insect that can move its head from side to side.

9

Would You Like a Mint?

What's your favorite food? A dung beetle's favorite meal is poop! Some beetles roll the poop away and save it for later. Others choose to make their home right in the poop pile. Lots of hungry beetles can make an entire pile of dung disappear in a few hours.

Super Stink

Stink bugs don't bite, but they sure smell bad! Stink bugs are found across the United States. They have **glands** that make a smelly liquid. When disturbed, they release the stinky stuff. So don't squish a stink bug unless you can handle the scent!

gland—an organ in the body that releases chemicals

13

Don't Let the Bugs Bite—Really!

Bed bugs really do bite! Bed bugs can hide in cracks all over your house. They come out at night to feed. If you wake up covered in small bites, you might have bed bugs! Don't worry, though. Bed bugs won't just show up at your house uninvited. They have to hitch a ride to get there.

Gross Fact!

Bed bugs can live up to a year without eating.

Boogers for Breakfast

You know some bugs eat blood and poop. But there are also bugs that eat boogers! The face fly lives on farm animals and feeds on boogers, tears, and spit. It also snacks on poop and blood. The feeding fly causes the animal to make more tears and boogers. The extra food is an invitation for more face flies to join the party!

How Many Legs is That?

Millipedes may not bite or sting, but they're still creepy! When attacked, millipedes curl up into a ball. Then they give off a stinky and sometimes poisonous liquid goo.

Think one millipede is icky? Try thousands! In some places, people seal their homes up tight to keep out the **swarming** millipedes.

swarm—to gather in a large group

Wasp Versus Spider

This match of might starts with a wasp called the tarantula hawk. She hunts a tarantula spider and stings it. The **venom** then **paralyzes** the spider. The wasp drags the spider back to her den.

Once at home, the wasp lays an egg on the spider. After hatching the young wasp starts eating the spider. It feeds off the stunned spider for as long as a month.

venom—a poisonous liquid
paralyze—to cause a loss of the ability to control the muscles

tarantula
hawk

tarantula
spider

GLOSSARY

digest (dy-GEST)—to break down food so it can be used by the body

gland (GLAND)—an organ in the body that makes natural chemicals or helps substances leave the body

mantid (MAN-tid)—the common name for a group of insects, including those with the scientific name *Mantis*; these insects have triangular heads and front legs used for grasping prey

paralyze (PAY-ruh-lize)—to cause a loss of the ability to control the muscles

swarm (SWORM)—to gather or fly close together in a large group

venom (VEN-uhm)—a poisonous liquid produced by some animals

READ MORE

Guillain, Charlotte. *A World of Bugs.* Chicago: Heinemann Library, 2011.

Shores, Erika L. *The Deadliest Bugs on Earth.* World's Deadliest. Mankato, Minn.: Capstone Press, 2010.

Siy, Alexandra. *Bug Shots: The Good, The Bad, and the Bugly.* New York: Holiday House, 2011.

INTERNET SITES

FactHound offers a safe, fun way to find Internet sites related to this book. All of the sites on FactHound have been researched by our staff.

Here's all you do:

Visit *www.facthound.com*

Type in this code: 9781429676120

INDEX